YES MAM!
YOUR MUSCLE AS
A MOTIVATOR!

Nicole Chaplin

NC KAIROS NEXUS, LLC
New York, NY
info@nicolechaplin.com
www.nicolechaplin.com

The quoted ideas expressed in this book (but not scripture verses) are not, in all cases, exact quotations, as some have been edited for clarity and brevity. In all cases, the author has attempted to maintain the speaker's original intent. In some cases, quoted material for this book was obtained from secondary sources, primarily online and print media. While every effort was made to ensure the accuracy of these sources, the accuracy cannot be guaranteed.

Scripture quotations are taken from:
The Holy Bible, New King James Version (NKJV)

Cover Photograph by: Anthony Djuren
Cover Graphic Design by: Jeremy Sumpter
Cover Photograph Enhancements by: Deborah Tiemi Tosetti

Book Edited by: Nikki Chaplin

ISBN: 1480178144
ISBN 13: 9781480178144

Hi Dennis, thank you so much for

Dedicated to my best friend.
The glow of your spirit touches souls where ever you go.
I thank God for your love and guidance.
I am your biggest fan forever.
To my Mom.

Believing in me. You're a complete gentleman 😊 Nicole Chaplin

Acknowledgements

I've met remarkable individuals along my journey to accomplishing this book. I thank God for his guidance and his blessings. Thank you also to my dear friends who have inspired and assisted me along my journey.

Arissa Horgan, Anthony Peralta, Anthony Djuren, Andre E. Enriquez, Bernadette Chitolie, Bob Hold, Brittanie Jones, Carol Burgos, Cindy Dorrejo, Christina Lewandowski, Daniela Cardillo, Deborah Tiemi Tosetti, Duane Kinoe Bridgeford-El, Eric Kabakoff, Gina Thompson, Janelle Echemendia, Janette Cervera, Jessica Cruz, Jeremy Sumpter, Joseph Candela, Kat Rivera, Kathleen Murray, Larn Cunningham, Lindsay Snyder, Lisa Bass, Lourdes Kearney, Maggie Farrell, Marcus Lewis, Michelle Cura, NOE (the artist), Pervis Taylor III, Shahreen Mehjabeen Read, Sonja Darby, Terry Piscitelli and

Wyclef Jean

To my loving family, friends, clients and mentors not mentioned above thank you and I deeply appreciate your continued support.

Introduction
What Really Matters

My desire for writing this book is to inspire those of you who've taken the time to pick up and read this book. I hope that by the time you finish reading these chapters you will come to see your body, in particular specific muscles of your body, in a brand new and exciting way.

I hope that you will begin to see and use each one of your muscles as a friend who's willing to remind and motivate you in some fresh, never before thought of ways. Yes, I do believe that every muscle of our bodies, with the right training, can become our life long best friend (LLBF).

I would like to first give you a brief history of what has shaped my life so far and by peeking into a little of my journey we can establish a special connection that will take us even further. My hope is that each of you in your own unique way will connect with my journey and the experiences I'm about to share, especially as it relates to the power of a thought, its effect on our bodies and on how far we excel in life.

My life so far has been filled with many rich, exciting yet challenging experiences and looking back I cannot explain how I managed to come through some of them. In a nutshell, my life has been far from rosy, rather it's been filled with more than its share of ups and downs.

However, even though I've had to live through some very negative and unhappy experiences, I constantly remind myself that ultimately I control the outcome. In those experiences in particular, when I catch myself buried into the negative aspects, I quickly switch to something more empowering such as what's within my control to handle.

I've learnt that the mental energy used to focus on the negativity of a situation would unconsciously undermine much of the spiritual and mental energy needed to achieve a positive outcome. It's the classic "glass half-full, half empty" way of seeing a situation. I learnt that it's my own personal choice on how I choose to see the glass.

When I'm seeing the glass as half empty I am choosing to focus on how much I lack control of the situation. But in seeing it half full, I am choosing to focus on how much control I still have. Best of all is to see the glass completely full and in some instances even overflowing. For what you believe is what you will achieve.

I was born and raised in Miami, Florida of Jamaican parents. My skin is chocolate, my lips are full and defined, my nose is broad and pronounced, and my natural hair is thick and strong. All that aside, I have come to realize that I am a divine creation of the Master Creator, the all-important One who's very proud of me, and none of the features I just described matter to him. To the Creator, I'm simply divine, "fearfully and wonderfully made." (Psalm 139:14). I'm chuckling inside as I write this because as far back as the second grade and even through most of high school I remember being called anything but divine. Back then, I did not know whose opinion really mattered most.

My difference made me self-conscious early on in my life. With very few exceptions, I was the only person with a dark complexion in almost every class and I felt it made me stand out considerably. My peers were mostly Spanish or Caucasian.

The consolation for me came in physical education (PE). I excelled there. I was faster, stronger and enjoyed having more stamina than most kids in my class. In my tender and naïve rationale I imagined that it was because I was of African descent. Or was it because I was so physically active being a cheerleader, track and field runner and dancer. Without even realizing it I was getting glimpses of what was to come, but more on this later.

My teeth weren't straightened until college when I got braces, but all the way back to elementary school, I had a very strong sense that how you looked mattered a great deal to many of my peers. My skin was constantly attacked by acne until nearing high school graduation, so that did not help matters in the "plus" column for me. So young, yet it seemed at the time, I was being taught that my darker skin somehow made me less worthy and perhaps less liked than others. At such a young age, I was already feeling like I didn't quite fit in, it seemed my self-esteem was getting pummeled from all sides.

As I grew into a young adult, I started experiencing more things, like being followed around by employees in department stores while simply browsing for clothes. Was I here to buy or to steal? Hmmm. Obviously, it depended upon who was being asked.

As I became more aware of how different I was, finding my own identity became more and more arduous.

Grade school was indeed a very challenging time for my self-esteem and I was relieved to move on from there. But high school was no better. As my physical body began to change and develop, I grasped harder to find some sense of self-confidence, but even that was nowhere to be found. By twelfth grade I had a boyfriend and was certain that somehow this would take away some of my anxieties. Unfortunately, I was still very insecure and so very wrong.

I tried my best to excel in academics, but this too became a challenge. It seemed I always had to study harder than my friends in order to pass my exams. I remember constantly asking myself, "How can school be so hard?" Even when I would study for hours, I would still score subpar test results. When I took the SATs for the first time, my scores were so low, I wondered how did I attend a solid year of prep classes and still score at rock bottom levels.

I knew full well my academic future depended on hitting a high mark on the SATs. The thought that I would not make it further than high school was simply unbearable. After all, college was where most people went to get a jump start on life, or at least figure out some sort of game plan.

I hadn't figured out what else there was to do with my life and the fact that I had no plan "B" was staring me squarely in the face. Not to mention that I felt it would be such a slap in the face to my Caribbean single mother who fully expected me to at least go as far as she did in college.

Introduction:
What Really Matters

I buckled down, with the single goal in mind of just doing well enough on the SATs to have my chance at pursuing higher education. At that point I noticed a slight shift had taken place in my thinking as most of my waking thoughts were now consumed with scoring as high as I could on the SATs. Getting into college was now my strongest motivation.

As a result of my new found drive and hard work, I received a scholarship to the University of Miami (Florida). I was elated. Unfortunately, my excitement was to be short lived. I was seventeen, and as it turned out, this was to be a defining moment in my life. The relationship with my boyfriend became violent.

One day outside our chemistry lab, he and I had an argument over whether I was cheating on him with his best friend Tirico. In his mind, the evidence of my cheating was that I was wearing Tirico's necklace. Before I could explain Tirico and mine's friendship to him, he reached over, grabbed the necklace and started to choke me with it. I tried to break through but the next thing I knew he sucker punched me in the face and I was lying on the ground with him sneering down at me.

Not one to cry and run, I got up, mustered all the force I had and slapped him right back in the middle of his face. My ego was at stake, my self-esteem was wounded and so I made a decision to defend both against this six foot almost two hundred pound high schooler, who would later be drafted to the NFL. I don't remember what happened next, but by the time the school security and principal arrived, my forehead was torn open and I was bleeding like a leaking faucet.

But that wasn't the worst part. The worst part was my expulsion from school. The episode almost caused me to lose my college scholarship. Needless to say the incident put an end to my relationship with "Rocky Balboa." Sadly, now in addition to my missing self-confidence I had heaped on more blows to my self-esteem.

The more I thought about the way my young adult life was starting out, the more I realized something had to change. Even though at the time I did not really know what that "something" was, I knew enough to realize that I had to change me.

At the beginning of the school year I was so focused on myself and how different I thought I was from everyone else, no wonder my grades were suffering. Gradually, as my focus shifted towards my grades, the pressure I felt about being different was no longer in my face all the time. I was feeling a little lighter about me. My grades were starting to improve.

I was embarrassed to have to take the SATs for the fourth time but I sucked it up. When I did this time, I reached my goal and fortunately I was able to attend the University of Miami. I was now entering my first semester in college and I began having a new outlook on my future. I decided to improve on my decision-making.

It had taken me some time to begin to learn from my mistakes but at least I was beginning to learn. I was realizing that if I go through something no matter how difficult, I can decide to learn from it and it can assist me with making better choices in the future. Moving forward I had made up my mind to do just that.

CHAPTER 1

M.A.M
Muscle and Motivation

*O*ftentimes the situations that life throws our way can look confusing and it's not clear where to begin to make sense of things. Still, you take comfort in the fact that since others around you seem to be doing a fairly good job of it, you can too.

Yes MAM! Your Muscle As A Motivator!

At times decision making seems easy, and the results are pleasant and as expected. Other times it seems as though we have more options than the squares on a Rubik's cube and the result can be unpleasant or disappointing. Making the best decision begins with using lessons learned from our past experiences, and calling on the wisdom of those we trust. As your decision making process improves, you find that you are now motivated to stay on the path of making better choices.

All through college I was never quite sure in which direction I should go with my life even though I was enjoying my major in marketing and minor in music business. However, or as long as I can recall, one of my strongest passions had been exercise. I've always had a deep appreciation for the human body and its miraculous way of serving us, by working around the clock. But it wasn't until I was an adult that I came to really understand how health and fitness worked in harmony as forms of personal therapy. I was beginning to appreciate how these two were connected in helping us enjoy a more wonderful life. Fitness felt like the one area of my life where I could take control over what mattered most. And so began my journey to follow my passion.

As my devotion to fitness and dedication to exercise grew I was becoming much better all around. Internally, my self-esteem was on the mend, and externally my health was getting better. This is one area where I was no longer at the whim of what others thought about me. My mind was becoming sharper, my physique was improving and I felt better from head to toe!

Principal Pillars

Exercise, when it is effective, is based on three basic principles:

Persistence
Energy
Resistance

Hmmm. Interesting. Then, would it be safe to conclude that these same three attributes could be used as a metaphor for the way we approach fitness, health and our lives overall. The answer, of course, is "absolutely."

The motivation system I'm about to introduce to you is based on using certain muscle groups to correlate with a "motivating principle." I call this method M.A.M, or

Muscle And Motivation.

You already have the muscles. I hope to bring it into a principle that works on another level to help you accomplish your goals. Motivation is something we all need in one form or another. Along with motivation you will need inspiration to live out your highest potential.

So from this point on, I invite you to join me as a fellow partner along this fitness and life journey. Partners in achieving a better life incorporating some of the principles I am about to share with you. Thank you for allowing me to be a part of your journey.

"Application and application alone is the only evidence of learning."

A.R. Bernard, Founder and Senior Pastor, Christian Cultural Center

CHAPTER 2

The Derriere
Balancing the Ego

*T*he derriere muscles are what props us up
when our feet need a rest, giving us cushy
support as we plop into a chair or lie flat
on our backs. These muscles are more commonly
referred to as "the glutes." They have been called
many names, such as the buttocks, the fanny and

the rear end. Actually, the glutes are made up of three muscles, the gluteus minimus, medius and maximus. Of the three, the gluteus maximus is the largest and most superficial.

Aside from providing much needed support for our bodies, the glutes are often used by men and women alike for less vital purposes. Yes, you guessed it, the derriere, well proportioned or not, can be used as an object of desire by many of us, and sometimes a source of envy by others. This is oftentimes the area that many women tend to focus their time and attention on improving, sometimes neglecting other areas. In fact, some may say that our culture is downright obsessed with a fabulous looking tush, if only for the sake of vanity.

I used the term "well proportioned," advisedly because what's considered attractive is according to the eye of the beholder. Nonetheless, many women strive for this well-proportioned derriere, if for no other reason than to look blazing in a pair of jeans. It's easy to get carried away with actions that do little more than feed the ego momentarily while neglecting to care for ourselves and others in ways that are more meaningful and lasting.

I'm Your Ego, Feed Me

Most of us aspire to enjoy the finer things in life, and with that we place a measure of importance on achieving material gains. This isn't a negative thing. In fact, the more you have the more you can share with others. It is healthy to push yourself to attain more as long as it does not become your all out aim in life, leading you to neglect nurturing a caring relationship with those who are dear to you, and even reaching out to others who need you in some fashion.

While we are on our path to getting the most out of life it serves us to seek to understand ourselves as individuals, and to remain grounded in who we are and what's important to us, not just doing something for the purpose of impressing others.

Striving for Balance

One day on the gym floor in front of the heavy weight area by the mirrors, I glanced at a member doing bicep curls. After some time he began to strain. The weight was clearly too heavy, yet he wouldn't put the dumb bells down. In the mirror this man was watching the man next to him, who was in turn paying attention to his own workout.

I watched as the first member began trying to outdo the second member in weight while doing bicep curls. The second member was doing bicep curls as well but seemed quite unwilling to participate in a weight lifting competition he didn't care for.

The first member was obviously struggling under the weight and soon after gave up because it seemed the weight was overpowering him. When the second member realized the so called competition was going on, he quietly moved to the other side of the mirror wall and proceeded with the rest of his workout. Now that this fake contest was no longer going on, I wondered if the first member thought it was worth the effort and the risk of being injured, and was the ego satisfied.

I must admit that I too have done similar things in the past. I have been guilty of being both gym member number one and gym member number two. Having observed the same behavior in someone else, it came home to me how our egos if not checked, can turn us into nothing short of a spectacle, and not an interesting one to say the least.

Our ego at times needs checking. Sometimes it can serve as a positive driving force in our own personal self-improvement. However, if we aren't at the same time working on our self-awareness, constant feeding of the ego can lead us to becoming shallow and superficial.

Many women perform the squat exercise to boost the appearance of their glutes and develop leg strength, which in turn supports their ego in a positive way. I will admit that looking great in your 501 Levis can go a long way to boosting one's self-esteem.

While it is very important to have a positive self-image and a strong body, it is just as important to develop your character on the inside. The ego requires the same balance. When given too much attention it can lead to a person becoming superficial. Yet, when not given enough attention your self confidence may be weakened.

The Ego has Landed

Wellness, in its simplest definition, means having a healthy balance of the mind, body and spirit that results in an overall feeling of well-being. I believe in displaying the best and healthiest body but the latter should be a part of the overall goal when deciding to live a balanced life.

The Derriere Balancing the Ego

I remember attending an event some years ago where the atmosphere seemed filled with all the attendees being on their "A" game. I recall looking around the room and it seemed that the majority of the young ladies seemed to look and dress like each other. The conversations were in full pitch as one woman would state how much she had attained in social status and immediately the next woman would try to outshine her. Egos were being matched against each other.

When I first arrived I felt confident of who I was and my plan was to relax and have a good time. But after the event got into gear I began hearing their conversations, and doubt myself and my accomplishments. I became nervous and anxious, even though prior to the party I was fairly content with where I was in my life.

On paper my resume didn't look anything like theirs, it sure did not measure up and my nerves were starting to get the better of me. My mind wondered what was I going to say when they asked me about my life and my accomplishments. I quickly moved into plan "B", retreating from the conversation, nodding and smiling when others spoke. Clearly, it felt as though I was not in their league.

As far as I could tell, the women did not seem conceited, in fact most had warm personalities but they couldn't resist playing a game of "name that material possession." Once someone stated their resume of luxury items, another woman would jump in to top her. And so back and forth the ego competition began, with this conversation taking up much of our time together it left little time for us to really check in and catch up with each other's well-being. The ego it seemed had an insatiable appetite that would never be satisfied.

I reminded myself that this was another example of what can happen when we allow the material aspect of our pursuits to take center stage in our lives. We live in a competitive world for sure, and most of us at one time or other tend to fall into the trap of becoming overly superficial. That is, giving most of our attention to our appearances and possessions and little attention to the person on the inside. In the midst of the material competition and the superficiality of it all, I wondered did we forget caring for the needs of the person within.

Maintaining a Healthy Ego

How will you know if your ego has exceeded its healthy threshold? Here are some clues you'll begin to recognize:

Fear of outcomes:

"What if this person is better than me?"

Comparing yourself to others:

"What if I do not have what it takes?"

"I can do that too, and better than you."

Taking offense to constructive criticisms, using statements similar to:

"How dare you think you can tell me…," or

"I know this already."

Embellishing the truth:

"I own this, I have that, I make this amount of money…"

The Derriere Balancing the Ego

One of the most effective ways to keep your ego in check is to strive to be your best without comparing yourself to others. Another way the ego creeps up on us is by the seeking of others' approval, or to gain an advantage at the expense of another. In such situations, it helps to be mindful of not always looking to see what you can gain from the situation or the person, but what can you give.

As you read in my introduction, I think the most important approval you need in life, is that of yourself. I believe your own self-approval is what counts the most in life, because that is all you have total control over.

Approving and accepting yourself will go a long way towards keeping your ego in check. The ego can make you overly focused on yourself. In this case, try to see how you can give or offer your hand and the focus will shift from it being all about you. Yes, a great looking derriere can be an ego boost but looks are only skin deep. Working on the person within and be giving of yourself to others is more meaningful and lasting.

"My ego is controlled enough that I don't have to be the focus."

Herbie Mann, Jazz Flutist

CHAPTER 3

The Rhythm
of the Heart

*S*cience has now discovered that every time
your heart beats, it sends an encoded
message to every cell in your body, updating
that cell about what you believe about yourself.
It is said that in the course of a lifetime the heart
muscle performs the largest quantity of physical

work in comparison to the other muscles in the human body. That shows the enormous strength of this muscle.

The human heart's power output ranges from 1 to 5 watts, compared to the quadriceps muscles which are significantly larger in terms of mass, and produce over 100 watts, but only for a few minutes at a time. So the heart which works continuously over an entire lifetime without ever pausing outworks all our other muscles.

What brings you excitement, creates a smile on your face, and challenges your mind in a healthy way? Is there something that you do as a hobby that makes your heart race? Your heart contains your desires and is strong enough to assist you in making your dreams come true as long as you persist in feeding your dreams with your actions.

Just as our heart muscle never stops to rest, so too our drive to accomplish our heart's desire should not stop until we see it through. Think of all we could accomplish if we went after each goal with such consistency as our heartbeat. Even though such complete consistency might not always be possible, it is certainly worth striving for. If nothing else, we can still use the uninterrupted rhythm of heart to remind us to keep striving for what we want, out of life.

Losing weight and being more consistent with our gym regiment is a goal for many of us. We tell ourselves, "this year I am going to work out six days a week for one to two hours a day, and lose a certain amount of weight by such and such date."

We often have good intentions but realistically the over-zealous approach rarely lasts and we all too soon lose the zest and the motivation to continue. Pacing ourselves is a more reasonable and realistic approach to go from crossing the bridge of goal setting to goal achieving.

The motivation within you has to be strong enough to fuel you in order to pursue each goal to completion, not just fire you up momentarily.

My Heart's Desire

Before I entered into the fitness industry, the music industry had my heart. I would listen to music every chance I got. When I purchased an album or a song I would research the producers, the recording studios, the songwriters, and others who were mentioned in the credits then pick which song I thought would be the artists' next single or biggest hit.

I think back on how I had such a deep interest in knowing as much about the music industry as possible. While enrolled in the School of Business I soaked up and enjoyed what I learned about marketing and the music business. I soon realized there was but a teaspoon full of opportunities in Miami to further my career in the music industry. For me, New York City was the best place to launch my career. I made the decision that upon graduation I would move to the Big Apple.

As my interest in music grew, it became my dream to work at a record label. During my last year at UM, I began emailing my resume to recruiters, labels, publishing companies, booking agencies, and anything attached to the music industry in NYC, consistently for eight months. I did not receive a single response.

Graduation was approaching and I was faced with a dilemma, even if I did receive an internship offer or a full time position, where in New York was I going to live? Well, neither opportunity opened up to me.

However, something cosmic seems to happen when you want something so bad and you take a dive of faith by putting all your energy into it. While at UM, I was a resident assistant, RA, on campus and became close friends with another RA, Leyla.

Leyla and I had a great deal in common. We were both of Jamaican heritage. In academics we both favored subjects such as algebra, calculus, geometry, and we eventually enrolled in a few classes together. As time passed we discovered that we shared the same goal of wanting to move to NYC immediately after graduation.

During spring break of our senior year while the majority of our friends were riding jet skis on South Beach's aqua waters or tanning in Cancun, we booked two round trip tickets to the city that never sleeps to look for an apartment that we could call home after graduation.

We had only three days to pull this off. Looking back the idea seems crazy but at the time nothing seemed impossible to us. We knew what our hearts desired. I was more nervous about the idea of moving then Leyla because she had discovered days before that her internship in Miami had blossomed into a full time position on Wall Street. While at the same time, I kept holding onto my dream with no job insight.

We took the trip to Manhattan in March, two months prior to graduation. Most of the snow was still piled up along sidewalks but the city was abuzz with excitement like I'd never experienced before. The first two days we scouted every inch of Manhattan tirelessly and excitedly and were shocked that almost every apartment we looked at was out of our price range. Even though we were prepared to settle for a smaller apartment, the few that we could afford seemed smaller than our dorm closet back on campus. Our spirits started to become weary, we knew how badly we wanted to move in together and find a place we could afford. In addition, time was ticking rapidly. The next day we would be back on a flight to Miami.

On the last day of our trip we lifted each other's spirits and started out again. We had one more place on our list. The apartment was located in a newly renovated area in Brooklyn, and once we saw it we knew it was for us! The size of apartment exceeded our expectations. It was freshly renovated, more spacious than the others we had looked at and had a lovely view of the city. We were more than excited and pinched ourselves that lady luck had smiled us in a magical way on our very last day.

Since Leyla and I had first decided we would move to New York together we had been saving our money and worked hard to come up with the finances we knew we would need to make this dream a reality. We graduated the second week of May and became official roommates the first of June. Our new address was the third floor apartment on 314 Hull Street in Bed-Stuy, Brooklyn, NY.

My desire to live this dream of moving to New York was so strong, I did everything I knew in my heart to accomplish that dream, never wavering, never losing faith. This was part one of my heart's desire, and now I was there.

Living on the Edge

Part two of my dream was to secure a position in the music industry. I was living in a comfortable and affordable apartment with Leyla who I knew and trusted, so in regards to my living conditions I felt at ease. There was however, one major problem, I did not have a job. Leyla was relying on me to have my portion of the rent and bills, and expected me to be responsible with having the money ready when they became due. Besides, I needed to take care of my own personal needs.

My "no job" situation started to worry me. No job meant no income. How was I going to pay my portion of the month's rent and all the responsibilities of living on my own? When I moved from Miami, I had a thousand dollars and a dream.

I believed in my heart I could make it in this new city, and I did not see any other option but to survive. I encouraged myself with the thought "where there is a will, there's a way." As much of a cliché as this statement is, it was all I had to work with at the time. But the nagging question kept staring me in the face, "how do I land a position doing something I want to do in the music industry?"

Looking back, I can see that right here I was being set up to learn a new and very profound lesson that I will keep close for the rest of my life. When you desire something with such intensity it will send out a frequency of like strength, tapping into and causing your higher power to send you assistance from somewhere in its own chosen way.

My assistance would come in the form of Tiffany, a friend from Miami, who had earned a summer internship at a major TV network in Manhattan. Leyla and I knew back in March, during spring break, that we had a place to live in New York, so we agreed that Tiffany could stay with us while she completed her summer internship.

While in Miami, Tiffany had met someone from Manhattan who was in the music industry and was vacationing in South Beach. Meanwhile, on our last days in Miami before moving to New York, Tiffany, myself and her new friend all had dinner one evening and she mentioned to him that we would both be in NYC at the top of the summer. June arrived and Tiffany was in NYC residing with Leyla and I, completing her television internship.

One night Tiffany came home and told me she kept in touch with the friend from NYC and that his close friend was looking for an assistant at a record label. She told him that his friend should interview me because I would be perfect for the job. Tiffany followed up, and two days later I had an interview at Geffen Records, a subdivision of Universal Music Group.

Upon walking into the building, I remember beaming with excitement as I walked in the lobby, hearing the music playing, and gazing wide eyed at the certified platinum and multiplatinum plaques on the wall. This was my first interview at a record label and I fully realized this was my shot. I never had an internship or any involvement in the music industry professionally, so what little I knew about the record business at this point was what I had learned from my minor in Music Business Entertainment courses at UM and what I had taught myself by studying album credits.

The interviewer was one of the Artist and Repertoire (A&R) Executives for the label. I tried my best to appear poised and calm while inside my heart was racing. There was little small talk, what seemed like endless questions, and at the end, I expressed my goal of learning as much as possible. He stated at the close of the interview that the position would be granted either to me or one other candidate.

Three days later I received a phone call and was told the position was mine. I was ecstatic! I had landed a position at a major record label. Another dream come true for me. Thank you higher power. I was now in the door. My career in the music industry was officially starting.

At Geffen Records I was exposed to premier artists such as Mary J. Blige, queen of Hip-Hop Soul, and Common, multi Grammy award winner and one of the most influential artists in the burgeoning self-conscious Hip-Hop scene. I now had the chance to be involved in the process of creating and promoting an album from beginning to end. This included the studio production, marketing, publicity, touring and everything in between. I was starting to apply the lessons I learnt in the classroom into real life situations.

After Geffen, I went on to work for Broadcast Music Incorporated (BMI) and delved into learning the ins and outs of music publishing. The highlight of my music career was working at Roc-A-Fella Records, home of music mogul Jay-Z, and super producer and rapper Kanye West. Under the tutelage of the label's

Co-CEO, Damon Dash, he helped cultivate my knowledge in the areas of marketing, new media, and promotion.

I had my own office with an inspiring view of midtown Manhattan. I was building strong business relationships with the label's artists, discussing their marketing plans and sharing creative ideas. My work gave me a tremendous sense of satisfaction that was hard to compare to anything else I had done up to that time.

While at the Roc-A-Fella, I discovered a new passion, that of artist partnership. This led me to work with a very talented lyricist, songwriter, singer and performer, an artist named NOE. He is still one of my favorite artists to this day.

My time in the music industry is quite memorable, and I acquired a great deal of knowledge. Most of my enjoyment came from cross marketing the label's artists and music with various products and building a successful reputable brand.

Our Desires

The heart holds our desires, and it can also to give us the strength we need to accomplish them. When we realize that our passions can be manifested into reality, that's when we start to believe and know that anything is possible!

"The starting point of all achievement is desire."

Napoleon Hill, Author, Think and Grow Rich

"I cheated on my fears, broke up with my doubts, got engaged to my faith and now I'm marrying my dreams.",
Unknown

CHAPTER 4

Biceps
Flex Your Muscles

The biceps are among the most famous muscles in the body. This muscle is one we can easily show off by making a fist and raising the forearm into a "V." Many individuals spend large amounts of time developing and shaping their biceps.

As kids we would often say to one another, "let me see your muscles," and would eagerly do the "Popeye the Sailorman" pose, proud to display a bump of a muscle no matter how small. It's cute but also a show of strength, and as kids it made us feel powerful, made us feel we could do anything. As children we feel fearless, but for some of us as adults it takes practice to regain that sense of fearlessness.

As we grow older we sometimes lose that spirit of innocence of showing off our strength, our inner power, and things at which we excel. As adults, we can gradually begin to shrink back from being proud of who we are.

So, what is your natural gift? Pause for a minute and think about it. What is innate to you that ignites your soul? It doesn't have to be career oriented but maybe a hobby and maybe through the hobby you may discover that in actuality it could become your career.

In my last career position before I moved to the world of personal training, I worked at a financial institution. My workday began at ten am. The hours were perfect for me since I was able to complete my gym routines before work and be at my desk on time. However, after the first few weeks, my heart became heavy and there was little if any joy in going to work.

At this point in my life it was the largest salary I had earned thus far. In addition to the work hours being ideal for me another bright side of the job was the great team members. Of the three co-workers I worked with in our department, I eventually became very close friends with two of them.

By month two I began to feel as if I was watching time pass me by. Inside I was slowly and silently wearing down. All too soon I knew I did not belong in that position, but I had taken it because I knew I was able to handle the role, and furthermore what mattered most to me at the time was that my bills would be paid. But going to work made me feel shallow day in and day out.

At this particular job all I did was what I was assigned to do and I left work each day with the same empty feeling as before. I gave my second best and not my all. My soul was aching, yearning to do something that could help others or at least make me feel like I was contributing to the world on some level by doing something more than striking computer keys all day.

Sitting at my desk, I would sometimes gaze at the bottom right hand corner of my computer screen and think to myself, "it's only 10:12 AM, I have seven plus hours left, and then tomorrow I will do this all over again, this can't go on much longer." Over the next two years I lived out that sentence many times over. I was gradually becoming more and more restless as I longed to discover and to live out my life's purpose.

The most joyous feeling for me had always been to assist others in reaching their goals. I longed to follow my purpose and each day that went by I felt as if I was leaving my gift under the Christmas tree. No one was being blessed by it because it was never unwrapped and was not being put to use.

On my second year anniversary at the bank, I decided to acquire the necessary certifications to become a personal fitness trainer. It was on a Monday when the light bulb clicked and I made up my mind to change careers. The wheels to launch out into something more satisfying were now in gear.

As fate would have it, on the Wednesday of the same week, my manager called a meeting and told us that our department was being downsized and they no longer needed us. The bank was going to outsource our work to another division outside of New York. That was my clearest sign to escape.

Not only did I decide it was time to move on and live my dream but I also had confirmation! I did not panic. I knew my time there was up and I felt good about my decision of becoming a personal trainer. At that moment, it felt like the stress of not being satisfied with my life's work had melted instantaneously. Tapping into our natural gifts will not only add greater meaning to our lives, but it will make our journey more enjoyable.

We have the ability to do anything we want. The only person holding ourselves back is the reflection in the mirror. When the bicep is flexed it displays a form of power. We have to use our internal force and execute our ideas and thoughts so they can manifest and serve as proof that we are capable of accomplishing any goal we set out to achieve.

I believe that television and media mogul Oprah Winfrey is powerful because with her achievements and wealth she is able to continuously help many others. In spite of her humble beginnings, she molded herself into becoming one of the most influential forces in broadcast media history. It largely stemmed from her undeniable belief in herself, and of course the help of many on her team.

Biceps Flex Your Muscles

Power cannot be obtained without, first, the belief that you can obtain your heart's desires. Once you are clear on a heart level about your goals, use your power to catapult your life forward and also help others follow suit.

"One reason so few of us achieve what we truly want is that we never direct our focus; we never concentrate our power."

Tony Robbins, Author, Peak Performance Coach

"*Too often we underestimate the power of a touch, a smile, a kind word, a listening ear, an honest compliment, or the smallest act of caring, all of which have the potential to turn a life around.*",

Felice Leonardo "Leo" Buscaglia, Author and Professor

CHAPTER 5

The Quads
The Fantastic Four

S ome fitness experts say the quads are the most powerful muscles we humans have. The quadriceps femoris is Latin for "four-headed muscle of the femur (bone)." These four muscles are located on the front of the thigh and are crucial for squatting, jumping, running and of course walking.

I admire individuals who use physical fitness along with their inner power to take control over what takes place inside and outside their bodies. I have been blessed to assist two clients in particular shed 70 pounds each, based on their dedication and willingness to leave their comfort zone. I noticed that during their metamorphosis these individuals became more independent and more aware of their inner strength.

This leads to a word called: change, simply meaning a transformation of some kind. Changing for the better requires discipline mixed with a healthy dose of faith, trusting that when we've done all we know to do, odds are that the outcome will work out to our favor.

Fear of moving out of one's comfort zone is one reason, for example, that a person who desires to move to a new city may stay put. They may resist taking the chance to explore a new territory. Being content is fine, but being fearful and complacent is not. If you are no longer striving for more because of the fear of change, then it may be time to look at the reason for avoiding change.

Just like the quads have four parts to it, there are four simple steps that we can take to develop the power within us to push beyond our comfort zone when faced with a road block.

Step 1: *Breathe. Yes, breathe.*
There may be times when you feel that you've done all you can, yet the problem still stares you in the face. This can sometimes lead to anxiety. Sometimes we lose our patience in a world that demands our attention immediately. We play many different roles within the course of a day and can become short tempered and lose the enjoyment of our daily lives.

Taking deep breaths allows you to settle your mind and think how to react to a circumstance in the best way. Breathe. Health experts agree taking deep breaths can assist in helping you cope with conditions that are closely related to and or exacerbated by stress.

Breathing slower allows our minds to re-cap and reassess what is going on in front of us. In situations requiring more critical thinking, breathing will enable us to decipher a better course of action oppose to following a quick, maybe even erratic reaction.

Step 2: *Look at your execution.*
One of the most attractive qualities a person can have is ambition tied to execution. It's wonderful to have a vision but without execution it will always remain a dream. Look at the steps you've taken so far, so you can better understand what's working, and what's not. Fixing what's not working may mean spending more time in that area, getting outside help, if necessary, or getting more creative in your approach.

The execution step is where you will begin to prove to yourself that you have everything it takes to be what you want to be. When you want something bad enough you'll go for it with your highest level of intensity. With your intensity in place, you will need to marry your drive with consistency, and you will be well on your way towards hitting your target.

Step 3: *Keep an open mind.*
Sometimes, your plans may need to change, because circumstances have changed. Be open to changing course if necessary. In some cases, you may even need to reach out to others for advice and be willing to listen to other points of views. Rather than being quick

to respond, listen objectively. This takes practice and is a sign of maturity and self-discipline.

Listening is not the same as hearing. Listen for the truth in the situation, not for what you want to hear. Try to understand what is being revealed to you without interjecting your own personal thoughts.

Listening means to absorb the information being given to you and being able to see someone else's perspective. This allows for better problem resolution while indicating to the other person that you are receptive to their point of view.

Step 4: *Learn to Let Go.*
Whatever life dishes out, you are the chief captain in your life and you can always work towards creating the best outcome possible. However, when you feel overly anxious and your concerns refuse to go away, you may simply need to let go knowing that there is a power much higher than yours looking after your welfare.

Let the four parts of your quads remind you of four steps you can take to get back on track if things in your life begin to fall off course.

"Should you find yourself in a chronically leaking boat, energy devoted to changing vessels is likely to be more productive than energy devoted to patching leaks."

Warren Buffett, Business Magnate, Investor, Philanthropist

CHAPTER 6

Take the Weight off Your Shoulders

*T*he forming the rounded contour section of the shoulder is called the deltoid muscle. The deltoids can be a representation of what bears us up when we feel like the weight of the world is on our shoulders. So often life seems to hand us more than our fair share.

Which of the following weights can you identify with?

- Trying to make a dollar out of fifteen cents

- Noticing that your children are not behaving as you would like

- Too many tasks on your plate at work to be accomplished in an unreasonable amount of time

- Looking for a job and still unsuccessful in finding one

- An unforeseen financial bomb occurs

- Health is beginning to become an issue

- Behind on this month's mortgage or rent

- Your significant other is not understanding you adding tension to the relationship

- Not being at peace where you are in life

We can all identify with one or more on the list above, leading us to feel that we are under too much pressure, especially when we are experiencing more than one of them at a time.

These are some of the emotional heavy weight bars resting on our shoulders that need to be handled or we might experience a mental and/or physical breakdown. If they are not addressed, we can start to feel downtrodden and even depressed.

Each of us has the ability to decide how we want to categorize events that take place in our lives. We've heard people say statements similar to, "I am so stressed my neck and shoulders are tight because of it." The pain caused by stress, especially in this region of the body, is commonly due to muscle tension. Many times the increased muscle tension aggravates a current condition.

Just like the hamster takes step after step trying to move forward on his little wheel, while in reality there is no progress, our minds often replay negative events over and over again resulting in the same outcome. The negative thoughts begin to take root in our heads and grow like weeds, or what we call stress. In addition to stressing about past events, we also fret about events that have not, and probably will not happen in the future.

Slowing down our minds and thinking of what action(s) the situation calls for is one step towards avoiding the "freaking" out reaction. Sometimes no action is the best action. To repeat the same event over and over, with no effort geared towards problem solving will only add to your frustration.

Stressing does nothing but rob us of precious time. Valuable time we can use to either plan a course of action or leave things as is and move on. Many times we stress over events that at first we think we have no control over, but on the second or third look, we can find creative ways to deal with them.

Earlier, I mentioned my close friend Leyla who was my roommate when I first moved to NYC. During our third year of living in Brooklyn she met her soul mate and they planned to get married and begin their lives together. It was time for us to go our separate ways. While I was delighted for her, I became scared for myself.

Even though I was in big city New York, I still felt at ease because I was living with someone I knew and trusted. But now I was going to be completely on my own. All of a sudden I became overwhelmed with questions like, "Where am I going to live, could I afford an apartment on my own, would I qualify for a loan to buy a small apartment, will I have enough for a down payment, how on earth is this going to possible?"

Each day I worried about my future living arrangements more and more. Fear continued drilling my mind. I tormented myself with this mental tornado for weeks. I would remind myself to relax, but I couldn't. Finally, I came to a point where I simply had to let go, telling myself "it's all going to work out." In that moment I took control of my emotions.

I started to put a plan together and went about researching apartments that were in my price range. The following weekend I hopped on the train and began scouting for my new home. I didn't have the slightest idea where the down payment to rent or buy a place would come from, but I kept going.

I arrived at the first address on my list and after a thorough inspection, I liked it enough and wanted to make an offer. I didn't have any savings so all I could do was call on my faith that the money would somehow show up. In the meantime, I phoned mother to let her know what my plans were, and also arranged with my close friend who was also a real estate attorney, Celeste, to draw up the contract and help me with the transaction. Almost like clockwork, many of the needed pieces began to fall into place.

The sellers accepted my offer and from that point on things started to move pretty quickly. Thankfully, financial help soon came in the form of a gift from mother. I was now one step closer to owning my own place in the Big Apple.

Take the Weight off Your Shoulders

Two of the pieces I needed to resolve my situation were now in place. In the end it was all working out even smoother than I expected. In fact, the apartment I was about to buy was the first and last one I had looked at. That night, I sat in silence, took some deep breaths, and wondered to myself, "What was the point of all the stress?" The mental anguish was a waste of time. Lesson learned. Do not stress.

Our shoulders can be used as weight bearers but within reason. We will experience pressure in our lives but we can convert such pressure into motivation for finding a solution. Starting to work on the solution with unwavering faith and trust in the divine higher self can alleviate unnecessary weight on our shoulders.

"Give your stress wings and let it fly away."

Terri Guillemets, Quotation Anthologist

CHAPTER 7

ABS
Standing by Your Morals

Good posture involves training your body to stand, walk, sit and lie in positions where the least strain is placed on supporting muscles during any type of movement. Our abs or abdominal muscles are special because they provide postural support. "Don't slouch", "walk

with your shoulders back", and "sit up straight" are some of the phrases we've heard growing up in order to have good posture.

As the abs provide postural support for the frame of our bodies, our morals are our support system for how we choose to live our lives. It is vital to our self-respect to stand up for ourselves and for what we believe.

Our morals and integrity are important components of our character. They should not be easily swayed but instead carefully guarded. If we begin a situation by compromising our beliefs in order to please or succumb to others' rules or ideas, later on down the line, it will be difficult to change back to our original beliefs. They will be accustom to the person you revealed to them initially which was not the true you.

Often, we bend our truths to be accepted by others. Some of us do this pattern our whole lives and live in the shadow of insecurity, constantly battling our true selves. However, we show our respect for self when we stand for what we believe. People may not like you for whatever reason, but our first principle is to respect ourselves. Standing up for yourself does not mean being combative or abrasive, it simply means living with honor and integrity.

I confess that I sometimes struggle with standing up for myself and what I believe in. But it's worth the effort, as the following incident with one of my clients proves. It happened one day on the gym floor, when a co-worker became loud and abrasive towards me, insisting that I pick up dirty towels strewn along the floor that he felt belonged to me. The louder he spoke the larger the scene became. I was training a client at the time, and I calmly told him I would not stand for his yelling, and if and when he could address me respect-fully I would listen to what he had to say. I kept it simple and short. He did not deserve more attention than that anyway. I did not allow him to push me out of my peaceful state of mind. With that I con-tinued training my client. Shortly after, he disappeared, and so did the offending towels, and there was no interruption to my routine.

A few hours later, I received the following text message from my client who I was training while the incident took place.

> "…My boss of 14 years is Dr. Jekyll and Mr. Hyde… one minute he's sweet, the next minute a cursing tyrant. He's just crazy. So I've been thinking of going to work elsewhere. Seeing you stand up for yourself today with such ease and peace was a wakeup call for me to reach for more. Thank you for being strong.…"

As I reflected on the incident, I was reminded how easily our actions may influence others, and how important it is to be aware of what we say and do. In the same manner that we can tear someone down with our words or actions, we can also do the opposite and uplift or build them up. But it takes practice, yes a lifetime of being aware of how we are acting each moment in time.

You can absolutely use your abs as a reminder to stand up for what is right for you. Your morals are the frame to your life's painting so be proud to stand by them in a positive and respectful way.

> "Respect for ourselves guides our morals,
> respect for others guides our manners."
>
> Laurence Sterne, Novelist and Clergyman

CHAPTER 8

Rock Hard Abs + Firm Lower Back = Balanced Core

*O*ur back muscles provide balance to our abdominals. The function of these muscles is to work with the abs to help stabilize the torso and give us a strong core. Some athletes call the core the powerhouse of the body. These muscles are essential for good posture while *standing or sitting. Good core strength is achieved by maintaining a balance of these trunk muscles. These often ignored muscles work in conjunction with our abdominals to provide balance to our physical frame. Similar to paying attention to our lower back muscles we also need to balance our overall wellness.*

We are all working on living a more balanced life, because like an overzealous child ripping through Halloween candy, we learned "too much of anything is good for nothing."

Three key components of wellness that lead to a solid personal pyramid are spiritual, physical and emotional health. In the busyness of life, we sometimes forget to pay attention to all parts of our lives, leaving some areas lower to last on the totem pole.

In the past I have been guilty of wanting to push for something so much that I neglected certain areas of my life, and did not recognize the possible damage that was being done to the parts I wasn't paying attention to.

As we focus on the role of the core muscles, they can remind us of being aware of not tipping the scale too much to one side which will eventually throw us off balance.

The Spiritual

At times, when the word spiritual is spoken thoughts of religion can make it daunting to deal with. In simple terms, the thoughts that your soul needs to feed on, to feel at peace with, to be able to think clearly, and to make the best decisions possible for your life is what spiritual health is all about.

Usually praying, meditating, sitting in a quiet space, listening to music, or reading about subject matter that is important to you contributes to your spiritual growth. As technology continues to advance, it requires more effort to dedicate to sustaining our quiet time or alone time necessary to feed the soul.

If we dedicate a few minutes each a day to be in solitude and take deep breathes and unwind it can assist us in letting go of negative thoughts that may have surfaced. The soul can also be cleansed when we take time to appreciate the little things in life like having fresh air and access to clean water. In the same way you give your time to others, you can balance things out by giving alone time to yourself.

The Physical

Keeping my body active on a daily basis allows me to maintain an upbeat attitude. I have the most fun when I do circuit training and cross fit. At one point I was exercising six days a week and sometimes I would bump it up to seven. I began losing sight that my body needed rest and recovery time, which are just as important as actual exercise. Because my routine became unbalanced, the inevitable happened. I burned out. My body shut down to the point that I could not exercise at all for six weeks. I became sick, weak and extremely lethargic.

With the decline in my body's rest and neglect of proper nutrition, my immune system was at a low point. Being out of balance, my mind and my body became two forces working against each other instead of in unison.

My mind was saying, "keep going, you can rest later," while my body was pleading to me the opposite, "slow down," it said, "I am drained, I cannot keep going at this intense level without rest." Where was the balance? There was none. I paid the price and learned my lesson the hardest of ways.

The Emotional

> I feel good, I feel nice
> I've never felt so satisfied
> I'm in love, I'm alive
> Intoxicated, flying high
> *"Emotions,"* by Mariah Carey

When we are in control of our emotions, it's a wonderful feeling. We can think clearly and enjoy the goodness of life, as Mariah Carey says in the first four lines of her song, "Emotions." Feeling emotionally high either because we are in love or because of something fabulous that's happened to us can be a very blissful experience. Our minds are in a position to think objectively and calmly deal with any issues as they arise.

It requires constant attention to where our mind dwells. Bad things happen, can happen and will happen, and yes bad things happen to good people. It is how life is at times. Perhaps if things were all good all the time, we would lose the feeling of appreciation for the good things.

One situation may be more difficult to handle than others but like the rain, difficulties don't last forever. Remember, emotions can be temporary. Don't let negative ones cloud all the good days you've enjoyed, or the exciting ones that may be just up ahead.

You can make the choice to balance your mind. Look at what's working for you, and decide to do something about the rest that's off track. Instead of spending enormous amounts of energy on what's not working, balance your life by distributing your energy over both areas. Take pride in all the efforts and the progress that you've made so far. Believe that whatever you may be going through will all work out in the end.

"Just as your car runs more smoothly and requires less energy to go faster and farther when the wheels are in perfect alignment, you perform better when your thoughts, feelings, emotions, goals, and values are in balance."

Brian Tracy, Inspirational Business Speaker

CHAPTER 9

Pump out
the Plan

In chapter three we discussed the heart's power and strength. Now we can address developing a plan using the heart to pump it out. For example, when starting a new gym routine, certain doubts may arise to keep you from reaching your goals. Some of the most popular reasons are:

- *I do not have enough time*

- *I do not have anyone to workout with*

- *I am not motivated*

- *My children need my attention*

- *My job consumes the majority of my time*

- *I'm just too tired*

These doubts and fears may not be the only reason we do not accomplish our fitness goals but any goal for that matter. However, when our health and fitness goals become top priority, we will somehow find a way to carve out time to dedicate to these objectives. Occasionally individuals ask me the question, "How do I find the time to make working out a priority?" My answer is simple "Start with a plan and if possible find someone to hold you accountable."

What can we do to find and sustain the strength to keep pushing forward regardless of the apparent forces pulling in various directions? First and foremost, any desire if it is to become a true goal must remain near the top of your priority list. It is also necessary to remind yourself regularly, even daily, of each particular goal.

Writing goals down and re-evaluating them on a consistent basis is vital. Reading them regularly is crucial as it becomes a constant reminder, and will help to focus your activities. For example, after hearing a song over and over before you know it, you can recite the words. The song becomes easily memorized and you enjoy singing along. The same principle applies to reading your goals daily. It becomes embedded in your mind.

Pump out the Plan

To move your goal from simply being a longing, you will need to transform your goal into a precise target, one that you can lock onto. For example, wanting to lose weight is a longing, but aiming to lose fifteen pounds within say three months is a specific target. Not having a precise target is one reason we sometimes do not accomplish our goals, as they often remain in the "longing" stage.

There are twenty-four hours allotted to all of us and the way to create time is to make the time you have work for you. This means scheduling out your priorities. Some things will have to take precedence over others. You will have to determine what items remain on your daily, weekly and monthly agenda and which items won't. A few years ago I had a routine that looked something like the following:

- Write my goals down

- Hope for the best

After New Year's Day, I didn't look at them again until the end of that year. After a couple years of this routine, I noticed a pattern. About half or sometimes less than half of my goals were coming to fruition. Why not all of them, or at least more than half, was the question I asked myself. The rest were just as important to me, so what was the problem? I set out to find the crack in my routine. After rethinking my approach, I realized that writing my goals down and reviewing them 365 days later was not enough.

There were no specific action plans, no reviews, and no updates. No specific ways to "pump out the plan."

I was not recognizing potential changes I needed to make throughout the year in order to accomplish my goals. It struck me that if Fortune 500 companies do quarterly reviews why don't' I do the same for my life.

Writing my goals down kept me excited at the beginning of the year but a few weeks down the road, I did not remember what all of them were. Therefore, glancing at them once a year was not a good plan. That upcoming new year I changed my approach. I repeated the first steps and added a few more:

- Quarterly reviews

- Identify areas needing improvement

- Delete goals no longer relevant or important

- Celebrate progress made so far

- Continue to execute during the upcoming quarter

The improved action plan assisted me tremendously. Breaking down my goals into quarterly chunks made them feel more achievable. My excitement was even greater because I had a three month window to work on each goal or parts of them and evaluate them. When I encountered a road block I would brainstorm with a close friend whose opinion I valued, and seek other courses of action to cross the bridge from goal setting to goal achievement. In the year following, I was able to accomplish the majority of my goals by the end of the year.

If you have someone that you trust and would like to share your goals with, by all means do so. In fact, it is vital to have a second or third person whom you can bounce your ideas and plans off of. Be sure you and the person you trust to share your goals with are on the same page. If the person is not a dreamer or visionary like you, they may unintentionally discourage you and this may weaken your desire and ultimate success in that area.

In order to achieve the success you desire, you will need others who will encourage and support you. In the beginning you may be solo and that is fine. Along your journey make the effort to develop ties with a trusted friend or advisor with whom you can share your thoughts and plans. He or she need not agree with everything you have in mind and want to do. However, if they can add constructive criticism and show you other possibilities and avenues you may not see, then even better.

Be careful of those you chose to have in your inner circle of idea sharing. There may be people who may not want you to win and that is fine because that is the role they have chosen to play. Do not waste time wondering why. It is does matter why and it is not worth your precious time and concern. The important point is to share your goals with those who are in your corner and who genuinely and sincerely want to see you succeed.

With your strategy in place and your growing support circle, go ahead, pump out the plan!

"Vision without execution is hallucination."

Thomas A. Edison, Inventor, Scientist and Businessman

CHAPTER 10

Calves
Often Overlooked but Vital

When individuals come to the gym more often than not the calf muscles are overlooked. The humble calf muscles do not seem to get much attention, but they are just as vital to supporting your overall body.

I once heard evangelist preacher Mike Murdock speak about where people focus their time and attention. He said it's amazing how we will spend our financial blessings on car washes, haircuts, new clothes, upgrades to our homes, weekly manicures and even personal training. However, when it comes to maintaining our mental health we neglect it by not paying much attention to renewing our minds.

One of the best books I've read is "Battlefield of the Mind," by televangelist Joyce Meyer. In it she addresses the importance of taking control of our thoughts. We invest in our bodies, our possessions, but often like the calf muscles the mind and spirit are neglected and not given much attention in terms of nurturing and renewing them.

Thoughts come into our minds like waves hitting sand at the beach, constantly, and it seems with no end. Some of these thoughts can be negative and detrimental to how we conduct ourselves, making it crucial to control what thoughts enter our heads.

How often do we give our minds exercise or adequate rest from these streaming wondering thoughts? When we lay in bed at night even though our bodies are still, our thoughts are running track relays: "What am I going to do tomorrow," "what did this person mean by that comment," "how much is it going to cost to do so and so." By the time we fall asleep, the alarm sounds and our daily routine begins again. No wonder we often start our day restless.

When do we give the mind the proper attention it needs to relax and refuel throughout the day? This part of the body needs downtime as well. Such downtime can be reading something uplifting, meditating, praying, walking in the park, going for a swim, playing a brain teaser game, or taking a power nap.

I noticed before I began meditating at the start of my day, I always felt rushed. I was eating breakfast on the go, sending text messages while getting ready, packing my bag and brushing my teeth almost all at the same time. I would then finish my triathlon morning with a nice run to the train. By the time I reached my destination I was fatigued and my work day had not yet begun.

The interesting thing is, once I began to take my time and spend the first few minutes of each day in mediation and sitting in silence, the tone of my day became better and better. The challenges that arose during the day would not push me around emotionally as much as before because I had programmed my mind to be at peace from the start of the day. I was in a much better state of mind and better prepared to handle the curve balls that life sometimes sent my way.

Life is not going to be rose petals and cupcakes all day every day but you will be able to live it with more joy if you engage yourself in an activity that you like that is peaceful from the minute the sun rises. This will help set a positive tone for your day.

As I write this book, there may be people at work waiting to receive that phone call or an email from a manager who has the power to make their climb up the corporate ladder happen. Then the meeting takes place and the subject is the possible promotion. The moment is finally here. But bam, they are met with disappointment instead of congratulations and are told the position is actually going to someone else. They say in their head, "I really did not expect to get the promotion any way, I felt it in my heart they would choose so and so over me."

This could very well be the reason they did not receive the good news simply because they truly did not expect it. Another word for this is self-sabotage. If we practice good mental habits, maintain positive thinking patterns and renew our minds, we will be able to control our thoughts and more often than not have better outcomes.

As Pastor A.R. Bernard says "You do not get what you want in life, you get what you expect."

When we neglect to develop our thoughts and our emotions in a positive way we run the risk of attracting friction and disappointment instead of joy and fulfillment. Don't spend mental time obsessing over negative events in your past, but review, re-evaluate and restructure a better plan to attract better outcomes in your future.

We are a machine, and the machine is composed of many integral parts that make up our bodies and souls. We can use the calve muscles as a reminder to be aware when we are possibly neglecting certain areas of our lives.

Life offers us its greatest joy through loving relationships with others, and its greatest fulfillment through achievement of our heart's desires. By believing, having faith and working diligently towards your goals you can have what you want out of life.

Calves Often Overlooked but Vital

Remember, the muscles of your body are tools that can work in harmony with your goals to provide the motivation to accomplish all you desire. You have what you need inside you to successfully move forward in all areas of your life. The spotlight is on you, go ahead and begin to use your muscles as motivators!

"Happiness and self-confidence come naturally when you feel yourself moving and progressing toward becoming the very best person you can possibly be."

Brian Tracy, Self-help Author, Motivational Speaker

"Let no one ever come to you without leaving better and happier."

Mother Teresa of Calcutta, Catholic Nun, Nobel Peace Prize Winner

Blessings from me to you.

I wish you love, success, joy,
fulfillment and balance on
your life's journey.

Photography Credits:

17488868R00046

Made in the USA
Charleston, SC
13 February 2013